SPORT AND POLITICS

Andrew Langley

Wayland

World Issues

Cities in Crisis
Endangered Wildlife
Exploitation of Space
Food or Famine?
Human Rights
International Terrorism
Nuclear Power
Nuclear Weapons
Population Growth
Refugees
Sport and Politics
The Arms Trade
The Energy Crisis
The Environment
The International Debt Crisis
The International Drugs Trade
Threatened Cultures
World Health

Cover: The Olympic flame being lit in the stadium at
Seoul at the opening of the 1988 Games.
Frontispiece: The USA and USSR battle it out on the
basketball court in the 1972 Olympic Games.

Editor: Jannet King
Series Designer: David Armitage
Designer: Gaye Allen

First published in 1989 by
Wayland (Publishers) Ltd,
61 Western Road, Hove
East Sussex, BN3 1JD, England

© Copyright 1989 Wayland (Publishers) Ltd

British Library Cataloguing in Publication Data
Langley, Andrew
    Sport and politics. – (World issues).
    1. Sports
    I. Title   II. Series
    796

    ISBN 1–85210–681–6

Phototypeset by Kalligraphics Ltd, Horley, Surrey
Printed and bound in Italy

Contents

1
The power of sport

What is sport? The question seems an easy one to answer. Sport is an activity in which people compete against one another. They run or jump or lift weights. They kick a ball, throw it about or hit it with wooden sticks. The aim of all these games is also simple – to beat your opponents.

But is it really so simple? Look more closely and you will see a darker picture. Sport today is always getting itself tangled up in scandals and controversies. Newspapers throughout the world tell lurid stories of football violence, drug-taking by athletes and cheating in every kind of game. Different nations argue fiercely about cricket and rugby tours and athletics meetings. All this international anger leaves behind it a trail of cancelled events, banned players and bitterness.

Sport is clearly much more than just a healthy form of exercise. It is a very powerful force in modern life. It brings thrills and pleasure to many millions of people who watch great occasions like the Olympic Games or football's World Cup. It also brings a lot of money to some of the people who play and organize it. But above all, sport brings glory, the glory of beating your opponents and being a champion.

Winning at sport is rather like winning in battle. The victor shows that he is better than his rivals. He gets gold medals, cups, money and fame, while the loser gets nothing. Just look at the delight of a football team which has just won a World Cup Final. They grin, leap in the air and wave clenched fists. Now look at the losers, with their glum faces and bowed heads.

Right: Tens of thousands of people gather to watch large sporting events, and millions more watch on television. Emotions run so high that supporters of the winning team feel as though they have won a personal victory.

Below: American football teams do battle on the pitch in a display of controlled aggression.

World sport has the power to provide thrills, money and glory. But this power is also its greatest weakness, for there are many people, apart from sportsmen and sportswomen, who want to use it for their own ends. Politicians, in particular, are eager to use sport as a weapon in their dealings with other nations. We don't have to look far to find examples of this. Political quarrels between the USA and the Soviet Union disrupted the Olympic Games of 1980 and 1984. Cricket and rugby tours to South Africa have been cancelled for purely political reasons. Individual sportsmen have been disgraced and banned for life because of politics. Sport may have suffered because of these incidents, but politicians have made the most of them.

Hitler's games

> Serious sport has nothing to do with fair play. It is bound up with hatred, jealousy, boastfulness, disregard of all rules and sadistic pleasure in witnessing violence: in other words, it is war minus the shooting.
>
> *George Orwell, 1950*

Trumpets rang out. A small figure, wearing an army uniform with a swastika armband, strode into the huge stadium. At once a massive roar of *Sieg heil!* thundered out from the crowd. The people had recognized their leader, Adolf Hitler. Thousands of right arms shot up to give the Nazi salute. Thousands of voices joined in the singing of 'Deutschland über Alles' ('Germany over all,' the German national anthem).

The year was 1936 and the setting was Berlin, capital of Germany. German troops were on the move in Europe. The shadow of world war was looming larger. So what was this grand occasion? Was it a Nazi rally, or a victory parade? No, it was the opening of the Olympic Games!

Since the Games had been revived at the turn of the century, they had been held every four years in different cities around the world. In 1936 it was the turn of Berlin. Hitler and his ministers saw that this was a golden opportunity to show the world how powerful and efficient they were. A vast amount of money and time was spent in making sure that the event was a glorious success.

A workforce of 2,600 men built magnificent new stadiums and houses for the athletes. Roads were widened and new railway stations opened. The city itself was cleaned up and decorated with flags and greenery. Parties, concerts and displays were planned. A massive new Olympic bell was cast. For the first time in the history of the modern Olympics, relays of runners carried a flaming torch from Olympia in Greece to the site of the games.

Hitler's Olympics, with their splendid new buildings and bright flags, were designed to glorify the Nazis and divert the attention of the world from the political situation in Germany. Only a year before, Hitler had passed a series of laws which took away many of the rights of Jews in Germany. Thousands of Jews were already being beaten, tortured and killed in concentration camps. Anyone who criticized the Nazis was liable to be imprisoned or executed.

Many foreign governments were deeply shocked at conditions in Germany, and tried to persuade their athletes to stay away from the Games. Dr A. G. Yahuda, a Jewish professor living in England, wrote: 'Nothing would so much weaken the position of the Nazis and shatter their prestige as the failure of the Olympiad.'

But the Games went ahead as planned and were a great success. Only one person spoiled Hitler's triumph: Jesse Owens, a black American sprinter. The Nazis believed that black people, along with Jews, belonged to inferior races. They hoped that the Olympics would prove this, with white, 'Aryan' athletes winning all events. The brilliant Owens won gold medals in the 100 metres, 200 metres, long jump and relay, easily defeating his 'Aryan' rivals and enraging the German leader.

The story of the 1936 Olympics tells us a great deal about the connection between sport and politics. Hitler used sport to make his own position stronger. Many foreigners were fooled into thinking that Germany was a friendly and

Right: Adolf Hitler turned the 1936 Olympics into a showpiece for his Nazi government.

The black athlete Jesse Owens of the United States won four gold medals at the Berlin Olympic Games and highlighted the absurdity of the Nazi's racist theories – a lesson Hitler chose to ignore.

peaceful place. But two years later German troops marched into Austria, and in 1939 the Second World War began.

What would have happened if foreign teams had boycotted the Games? Certainly it would have been a blow to Hitler's pride. It might also have drawn the world's attention to the appalling way in which Jews were being treated in Germany. The athletes had a clear choice. They could either ignore politics and go to Berlin, or they could make their own political point by staying away. It is a choice which has faced many sportsmen and women ever since.

German athletics are, in the complete sense of the word, political. They are the business of the state.

Kurt Münch, writer of Nazi propaganda, 1935

There are a lot of well-meaning busybodies who are trying to mix sport with politics. All I have to say to them is, 'Hands off sport, politicians.'

Sir Noel Curtis-Bennett International Olympic Committee, 1936

2 Sporting development

Most sorts of diversions in men, children and other animals, are an imitation of fighting.

Jonathan Swift, 1711

Sport has been mixed up with politics ever since it began. In fact many kinds of sports probably grew out of politics in the first place. The Olympic Games, for example, were founded in 776 BC simply to bring about peace. For years the different tribes and city states of Greece had been at war with each other. The Games brought them all together at Olympia, where their urge to fight was used up in running, boxing and jumping.

Other sports developed in much simpler ways. Some people, including the ancient Britons, used to cut off the heads of their defeated enemies and kick them about in a gruesome form of football. Another version of the game, complete with tackling and passing, was played by Roman soldiers as part of their training.

In these cases, sport was an important part of ancient life because it was very like war. On the one hand, it taught people valuable skills to help them survive. Anyone who was good at running, swimming and fighting had a better chance in life. On the other hand, sport was a means of using up people's aggressive instincts and easing tensions. Hitting a ball is better than hitting another person!

Many sports developed out of religious ceremonies. Tribes in the Assam region of India used to hold a tug-of-war contest once a year. The teams stood on opposite sides of a river, one representing the forces of good, and the other, the forces of evil. The result showed what would happen in the coming year. If the evil team won, the people were in for a hard time.

The Native Americans played games with sticks and balls as religious rituals. Here is a form of lacrosse, called baggataway.

Games were also played to please the gods of harvest and hunting, and to ensure a good supply of food. In North America, the Makah Indians played a kind of hockey, with sticks and a ball, at the beginning of the whaling season. In Mexico, the Mayan people built huge ball courts for their own special game, an precursor of basketball. The losers were often killed as a sacrifice.

Games such as these were vital to the everyday life of people long ago. Then, gradually over the centuries, the original reasons for them were forgotten. People went on playing them just for pleasure, and they became pastimes instead of ceremonies or battle celebrations. For a time, sport and politics went their separate ways.

Below: Eight centuries ago, the Mayan people of Mexico played a game called 'thachtli', which resembled modern basketball.

Empires and umpires

> Play up! play up! and play the game!
> *Sir Henry Newbolt, 'Vitaï Lampada'*

The game of cricket was invented in England. Why is it now a major sport in the West Indies, India, Pakistan and Australia? How did basketball get all the way from North America to the Philippines? Why does the European game of football have such a fanatical following in South America?

Sport has spread around the world in surprising and unpredictable ways. Cricket, for example, travelled far across the oceans with the British empire-builders of the eighteenth and nineteenth centuries. British settlers quickly formed cricket clubs in Australia, and the first recorded match took place in Sydney in 1803.

The scoring Table

Coming out

General view of the match

A Farsee Cricketer

The people of India learned the game from the British sailors and soldiers who were sent out to govern them. It soon became the most popular sport in the land. Later, one Indian was heard to remark: 'The finest legacies left us by British rule are the English language and, even more precious, the game of cricket.'

Cricket took longer to get going in another part of the Empire: the West Indies. This was largely because most of the black population were slaves until the system of slavery was abolished in 1833. And it was not until the end of the century that they had the time to develop their love of the game. Before long, cricket was being played everywhere – on beaches and in parks and back streets.

It is a strange fact that cricket has only ever been widely popular in countries which were once part of the British Empire. North Americans, for instance, found it too slow for their taste. So they developed their own kind of bat and ball game, which turned into baseball. They in turn took baseball to nearby nations where the American influence was strong, such as Mexico, Cuba and Puerto Rico. Basketball,

A cricket match in 1878 between an Indian team and their British rulers.

another American invention, is now the most popular sport in the Philippines.

The spread of these sports was obviously linked with politics. The ruling nations took their favourite games with them around the world and encouraged the local peoples to play them as well. In this way they were forming a closer bond between the colonies and their 'mother country'. The rulers also believed that playing team games would encourage the indigenous people to work together peacefully.

Football was different. Its rise to become the most popular game in the world had little to do with politics or empire building. Businessmen and other travellers from England began by playing it in Europe, where it caught on very quickly at the beginning of this century. Famous clubs like AC Milan and Bayern Munich were actually founded by Englishmen. From Europe, football hopped over the Atlantic Ocean to South America and by 1930 Uruguay was hosting (and winning) the first World Cup.

Cricket was introduced into the West Indies in the last century by the British. Today it is played with great enthusiasm wherever a flat surface can be found, which is one reason why the West Indian team is the best in the world and regularly beats the English team.

But not everybody liked football as they found it. Some countries developed their own individual versions. Rugby union and rugby league spread, like cricket, to countries governed by the British. The Americans, Canadians and Australians invented different rules, which became very popular. Older versions of soccer are still played in Ireland, South Wales and Cornwall.

A sporting world

At the beginning of the twentieth century, people were able to travel long distances more easily and quickly than ever before. Sports teams could take a train across Europe, or a steam ship to the USA or Australasia. Eventually, jet aircraft and motor coaches made these trips faster and more comfortable still.

All this had a huge effect on sport, which became truly international for the first time.

Below: Uruguay's winning goal against the Argentinians, in the final of the first World Cup, held in Uruguay in 1930. The English and other Europeans had refused to compete.

Cricket teams from as far apart as England, Jamaica, New Zealand and India made regular visits to each other. The Davis Cup competition for tennis was founded in 1900, and within a few years it was being contested by nine different countries. Tennis stars from all over the world flocked to play in the national championships in Wimbledon, Paris and New York.

But two sporting events in particular were destined to grow greater than all the others: the Olympic Games and the Football World Cup. The Olympics were revived in 1896 after a gap of some 1,500 years. Only 311 athletes, from thirteen countries, came to the first modern Games in Athens. Eighty-eight years later, at Seoul, South Korea, there were around 12,000 athletes representing 160 nations.

The first World Cup was held, to many people's surprise, in Uruguay in 1930. The surprise was felt largely in Europe (and especially in Britain), which believed itself to be the real home of football and could not see why such newcomers as the South Americans should be the hosts. The reason was a political one, for Uruguay was celebrating the centenary of its independence. All the same, the English and many other European teams refused to compete.

By the time the Second World War broke out in 1939, sport was making a lot of headlines and a lot of money. As the big international events became established, they attracted an enormous amount of public attention. It was not long before politicians began to sit up and take notice as well. We have already seen how Hitler took over the 1936 Olympic Games and turned them into a vast public relations stunt on behalf of the Nazis. Now that sport was big business, unsavoury episodes like that were to become all too frequent.

Below: Football is a national sport in many Central and South American countries.

The pressures of television

The history of sport since 1945 has been closely bound up with the explosion of the television industry. TV cameras have attracted a massive new audience for most types of games. In 1936, a few hundred Germans were able to watch live pictures of the nearby Olympics. In 1980, more than 1,000 million people throughout the world sat glued to their sets watching the Games in Moscow. The potential television audience for the Seoul Olympics in 1988 was 2.5 billion people (over half the world's population).

Today sport fills our screens. Safe in our armchairs, we can be spectators of Test cricket, football internationals, tennis championships, all-night snooker games and Grand Prix motor races. In the USA, sport can be seen at any time of day or night on a channel which shows nothing else. During any weekend in the season, fans of American football can watch non-stop live games for more than twenty-four hours at a time.

Television, as any politician knows, is a very powerful medium, and it has changed the face of sport for ever. To start with, it has brought wealth. TV companies are prepared to pay massive fees for the right to cover important

Television coverage has greatly increased the audience for sporting events, creating a new breed of superstar. It has also increased the prize money on offer.

matches. The money goes to organizers, agents and, of course, to the stars themselves, many of whom have grown very rich. Golfer Greg Norman earned more than $650,000 during the 1986 season, and in 1989 boxer Mike Tyson was paid $9 million for fighting Frank Bruno.

With so much money flying about, it is hardly surprising that amateur, or unpaid, players began to disappear from the scene. For instance, when the Wimbledon tennis championships were opened to professionals in 1968, very few amateurs enjoyed any success. In cricket, the distinction between amateur and professional had been abolished in 1963.

Money has also talked in sports which have remained resolutely amateur. Even today, athletes and rugby union stars are barred from receiving payment for their performances. But there is nothing to stop them from setting up trust funds which can be used after their retirement. Amateurs can also gain huge payments for advertising products such as running shoes, swimwear and sweatbands.

But in return for their money the television companies demand entertainment. And entertainment means star sportsmen and sportswomen doing remarkable things. Top athletes are now under enormous pressure not simply to perform well, but to win at all costs. It is no coincidence that scandals about cheating and violence on the field have become far more frequent in recent years. Money and television fame have made players so desperate to win that they are prepared to ignore the rules of their sport.

The most dramatic example of this came during the 1988 Olympics in Seoul, after millions had watched Ben Johnson win the 100 metres final. Shortly afterwards it was found that he had taken forbidden drugs to improve his performance, and he was stripped of his gold medal. The use of such drugs is not just against the rules and spirit of sport. It can also cause long-term damage to an athlete's body. In spite of this, many sportsmen and sportswomen are prepared to take the risk.

Thanks to television, sport has become an increasingly powerful influence on our lives. And that, in turn, has made it attractive to politicians and opinion-makers. Presidents and ministers are anxious to be seen playing golf in celebrity tournaments, or shaking hands with famous footballers. They hope that some of sport's glamour will rub off on them.

It is quite normal for athletes to advertise brand names on their clothes. A close-up television shot of the winner means that the name is seen by millions of viewers.

Below: Ben Johnson, the disgraced Canadian sprinter, being hounded by reporters on his way home from the Seoul Olympics in 1988.

3 Politics comes first

Like us, the ancient Greeks held their Olympic Games every four years. They did this successfully for more than eleven centuries. The modern Olympics have been going for less than one century, yet already they are bogged down by political quarrels. Scarcely a meeting goes by without some kind of controversy. To many people, the Games are a symbol of the unavoidable and unhappy link between sport and politics.

How sad this would have made the Baron de Coubertin. When he re-started the Olympics in 1896, he had high hopes for them. He wanted athletes to compete as individuals, and not as part of a national team. All that mattered to the Baron was that they took part, tried their best and behaved in a fair and sporting manner.

The early meetings passed off cheerfully enough, with a few minor difficulties soon sorted out. But by 1936, the year of the infamous 'Nazi Olympics', the pure spirit of the Games had become cloudy. The real trouble began in 1956 at Melbourne. For the first time, nations threatened to withdraw for reasons that had nothing to do with athletics.

> The most important thing in the Olympic Games is not to win but to take part, just as the most important thing in life is not the triumph but the struggle.
> *Pierre de Coubertin, founder of the modern Olympic Games, 1896*
>
> Today, thanks to the Olympic Movement, countries with very different political, religious and social views can come together in peace to compete in sport . . . It is not the duty of the Olympic Movement to encourage revolution or effect changes in a government's policies.
> *Lord Killanin, President of the International Olympic Committee, 1972–1980.*

Below: A painting based on a photograph of the start of the 100 metres race at the first modern Olympics, held in Athens in 1896 – a meeting untroubled by politics.

The bloodstained flat in which members of the Israeli team were held hostage and two of them were killed.

The Egyptians stayed away in protest at the English and French seizure of the Suez Canal Zone. The Chinese stayed away because the Taiwanese had been allowed to compete. (Taiwan then claimed to be the true Republic of China.) But the Hungarians surprised everybody by deciding to go to Melbourne, in spite of the fact that Soviet troops had invaded their country earlier that year. As bad luck would have it, Soviet and Hungarian teams came face-to-face in a water polo match and there was an ugly brawl.

After this, political gestures became much more frequent. The most horrible and tragic of these occurred in Munich in 1972. A group of Palestinian terrorists broke into the sleeping quarters of the Israeli team and took them hostage. They killed two of them before being allowed to leave with the hostages for the airport where they wished to board a plane to take them to the Middle East. At the airport there was a gun battle, and the remaining hostages and the terrorists all died.

Should the Games have been halted at once, out of respect for the dead? This was a decisive moment for the whole Olympic Movement. If the Games were called off, they might never happen again. The athletes of the world would have no great meeting to look forward to where they could compete with each other and make friends. Coubertin's Olympic ideal would have been destroyed by political fanatics.

But if the Games continued, there were two equally large problems. One was that it might seem insensitive to the feelings of the Israeli team and the families of the murdered athletes. Surely death was a more important matter than sport? The other problem was that the Games would simply grow more and more politicized year by year. If arguments and tragedies like this were to dog the meetings, Coubertin's ideal would be destroyed anyway.

In the face of these insoluble questions, the International Olympic Committee decided to carry on and, after a memorial service in the main stadium, the competition continued. The president of the IOC, Avery Brundage, was firm in his beliefs: 'We cannot allow a handful of terrorists to destroy this nucleus of international co-operation and goodwill we have in the Olympic Movement.' In other words, he would not give in to blackmail.

Below: A memorial service was held in the Olympic Stadium for the murdered Israeli team members, after which the Games continued.

But although there were no more tragedies like Munich, the problems got worse. The 1976 Games in Montreal were spoiled before they had even opened, by the refusal of twenty-two African countries to take part. They were protesting against the New Zealanders, because that country's rugby team had just toured South Africa. The African countries felt that anyone who went to South Africa was supporting the system of apartheid.

The Olympics of 1980 were held in Moscow, and caused an even more furious row. For in December 1979, the Soviet government had airlifted 5,000 soldiers into Afghanistan. Others had soon followed, and the affair turned into a bitter and bloody occupation. This time it was the turn of the USA to boycott the Games. Orders for this came from President Jimmy Carter himself, who said: 'Our decision is irrevocable. We will not participate.'

This, of course, left a gaping hole in the list

The cuddly Russian bear, symbol of the 1980 Moscow Olympics, gave no hint of the political disagreements that had led to the United States boycotting the event.

of competitors. American athletes would certainly have won many gold medals if they had attended, especially in the sprinting, swimming and boxing events. Their absence, it seemed, would ruin the Games as a worldwide competition. Yet the Olympics went ahead and were a huge success. The old magic survived all the controversy.

Four years later the USSR and other nations of the Eastern bloc took their revenge and stayed away from the Games in Los Angeles. It was a pure case of tit-for-tat. Once again, many of the finest athletes in the world were absent from the Olympics. Once again, the Olympic Movement seemed on the verge of splitting up. And once again, as soon as the competition started, these problems were forgotten. World records were broken, heroes and heroines were made, and millions of thrilled television viewers around the world sat glued to their sets.

By 1988 the Americans and Soviets had begun to patch up their quarrels. Might there, for once, be a harmonious Olympics? Unfortunately not, for the Games were due to take place in Seoul, the capital city of South Korea. Since 1953, Korea had been divided into two parts. Now the government of North Korea was jealous of the honour given to South Korea. It demanded that some events should be held in the North. Other Asian nations supported the demand. After a lot of wrangling, the Games went ahead, as planned, in South Korea. Disaster had been averted, but only just.

I was angry at the Soviet invasion of Afghanistan, and I knew that sport and politics could not be kept apart, however pleasant it would be if they could. But I thought the Games boycott was a dreadfully weak gesture.
Sebastian Coe, gold medal winner in the 1,500 metres at the 1980 Olympics

Below: The North Koreans were anxious to share in the staging of the 1988 Olympic Games, a right granted to the South Koreans. In the months leading up to the Games South Korean students demonstrated against their government's refusal to negotiate with the North Koreans on this and other political matters.

Sport strikes back

The Olympic Games are the most famous sporting event in the world, and because of this they have attracted more trouble than any other event. Political gestures have damaged every one of the last six meetings. It seems that politics has won in the end and athletics has lost out yet again.

But is this true? Each time the Games may have been affected by boycotts and arguments, but they still carried on and were a resounding success, with performances that will be treasured for a long time. No-one who saw them will forget the brilliant victories of Alberto Juantorena in 1976, Said Aouita in 1984 or Florence Griffith-Joyner in 1988. Sebastian Coe, a winner in Moscow and Los Angeles, wrote later: 'Games are remembered for who was there, who competed and who won medals – not for the athletes who weren't able to turn up.

The same thing can be said of other international contests. Take, for instance, the football World Cup, which has been plagued with political troubles ever since it began in 1930. Before the 1970 finals in Mexico, two neighbouring nations, El Salvador and Honduras, had played a dramatic qualifying match. When El Salvador won in the final minute, there was a riot. It went on for several days along the border between the two countries. When the smoke and shouting cleared, over 3,000 people lay dead.

In this instance, sport had been used as an excuse for starting violence between two nations who were already hostile to each other. The result had been horrific. Yet today few people outside Central America remember the carnage. Nor do they recall that the North Korean team withdrew from the competition because they refused to play against Israel. What lives in the memory is the football itself – and particularly the joy of the Brazilians as they won their third World Cup.

This doesn't mean that tragedies and other world events do not matter. It simply underlines the fact that sport can be a very powerful force. The thrill of great sporting deeds is so strong that it captures people's whole attention and kindles their imaginations. Sometimes this force can seem stronger even than politics.

Although boycotts of sporting events are an effective way of making a political statement, the enduring images are not of the gaps created by absent athletes, but of the great sporting moments, such as 'Flo-Jo' winning the 100 metres in the 1988 Olympics.

As we have already seen, the magnificent running and jumping of Jesse Owens enraged Hitler at the Berlin Olympics of 1936. He considered black people to be inferior to whites. Yet the German crowds loved Owens and cheered him wildly whenever he appeared. And Luz Long, the German champion whom Owens defeated in the long jump, became a good friend of the American.

This kind of comradeship can make a mockery of political divisions and international hostilities. On any day during the English cricket season, you can see West Indians and South Africans playing alongside each other in county sides. Yet the South African team is banned from the Test arena, and the West Indian team has never played it.

During the past decade, Argentinian footballers, Ossie Ardiles and Ricardo Villa, have played for English clubs. They have been very popular and very successful. Yet in 1982 British and Argentinian troops were locked in battle over the Falkland Islands, and even today the issue has not been settled.

This breaking down of barriers can be seen even more clearly in non-team games such as tennis. Here, each player is competing as an individual, and not on behalf of a country. South Africans, banned from most team games throughout the world, are accepted without question on the tennis circuit. Players from Communist nations, such as Czechoslovakia, are matched against Americans and Australians without a hint of political controversy.

The same harmony can be seen in sports as different as Grand Prix motor racing, golf, show-jumping, table-tennis and boxing. The stars are treated as individuals, and judged on their skills as athletes. But as soon as they become part of a national team, then the political barriers go up.

Below: The Argentinian Ossie Ardiles (in white) played for the English team Tottenham Hotspur both before and after the conflict over the Falklands which brought Argentinian and British forces into open battle.

4 Sport and racialism

them of international cricket, rugby, tennis and other sports would encourage them to reform their unjust society. The movement to ban South Africa from world sport has grown in three decades into a massive and far-reaching organization.

> The only aim worth fighting for is total racial integration at all levels, and the only way to achieve this is by total isolation. And it will work. South Africa is sport mad.
> *Sam Ramsamy, chairman of SANROC, the South African Non-Racial Olympic Committee, 1989*

> We feel we should have the right to play our sport wherever we like. Nobody agrees with apartheid, but I am a sportsman, not a politician, and I don't see that my not going will make any difference to the system.
>
> *Peter Winterbottom, English rugby player, 1989*

When we begin to talk about sport and politics, one name looms above all the others: South Africa. Since 1948, South Africa has lived under the system of apartheid, or separate development for whites and non-whites. White people govern the country, control the armed forces and own most of the wealth. They also make up all (or nearly all) of the major sports teams.

Apartheid has made South Africa a deeply unpopular nation. Foreign governments have called time and again for the system to be abolished, but in vain. They have also tried many ways of bringing pressure to bear on the South African leaders. One of the most successful of these has been to restrict sporting links between South Africa and the outside world. Sport is an important part of life for many white South Africans and it was hoped that depriving

Below: People outside the rugby ground at Twickenham in 1969, protesting at the appearance of the South African team, the Springboks.

The English cricketers who went to South Africa in 1982 were anxious to show that they coached black, as well as white, children. Critics pointed out, however, that such gestures did not solve the deeply rooted problem of apartheid, which affects every aspect of life in South Africa, not just sport.

The story of South Africa's sporting isolation begins in 1960. There were protests during the Rome Olympics that the South African team contained not a single black person. As a result, South Africa was not invited to attend the next Games in Tokyo, and has never been invited since. In the same year, a South African cricket team toured England, and found anti-apartheid demonstrations wherever it went.

By 1968 the doors were shutting fast on apartheid. The South African tennis team was expelled from the Davis Cup (a competition founded to promote friendly relations between nations). Then, when a Cape coloured cricketer named Basil d'Oliveira, who was by then a British citizen, was selected for an English team touring South Africa, the South African Prime Minister objected strongly: 'It's not the MCC team. It's the team of the anti-apartheid movement.' The tour was cancelled.

The South African rugby side which toured England in 1969 met fierce opposition from demonstrators and politicians. A cricket tour to England a year later was cancelled after pressure from the British government. South Africa's last cricket Test Match finished in the same year (just when, ironically, it had built up its finest ever side). The last tour by a British Lions rugby team took place in 1980. The wilderness years had begun.

But South Africa was not completely out in the cold. Since 1980 several private tours have been organized. An unofficial English cricket side arrived in 1982, to be followed by a Sri Lankan side and then two tours by a team of West Indian players. Individual cricketers and rugby and tennis players went to South Africa as paid athletes and coaches.

For many years the anti-apartheid movement has been trying to block such visits, so as to leave South African sport utterly isolated. Organizations such as SANROC (the South African Non-Racial Olympic Committee) and the non-white South African Cricket Board have urged all foreign sportsmen and sportswomen to stay away from the country. The United Nations has backed them up by compiling a blacklist of those who maintain sporting links with South Africa. Teams and individuals on that list are themselves punished by being banned from competing with other countries.

All this came to a climax during 1988 and early 1989. England was planning a cricket tour to India, but the Indian government refused to give visas to eight of the players because of their South African connections. The tour was called off, and another one, to New Zealand, hastily fixed up. This too was cancelled when Pakistan threatened to call off its visit to New Zealand if England was there.

Below: Most golf courses in South Africa are reserved for whites only – unless the black person is the caddy carrying the golf bag.

The anti-apartheid movement, strongly backed by the West Indies, Pakistan and other black nations, now had the upper hand. At the beginning of 1989, the International Cricket Conference bowed to the inevitable. It ruled that any cricketer who had sporting contact with South Africa would not be selected for international teams for at least three years. Shortly afterwards, the International Rugby Board imposed the same rules on its players.

The results of exile

> All our actions must be in line with the general effort to bring about a non-racial society. We must act in line with all the political organizations committed to bringing about change.
>
> *Sadiq Emeran, president of the South African Cricket Board*

Has this international outcry improved the lives of black and coloured people in South Africa? Has it had any effect on apartheid at all? On the face of it, the answer seems to be – very little. The South African government shows little sign of dismantling its hated system, or of giving non-whites a say in the running of the country in which they form a large majority of the population. Non-white people are still treated as second-class citizens.

Even on a sporting level, the situation is bleak. A report prepared by the Human Science Research Council shows that non-white sportsmen in South Africa are still very badly off. The report discovered that the following facilities were reserved for whites: 84% of cricket grounds, 73% of athletics tracks, 92% of golf courses, 96% of squash courts.

The authorities in charge of South African sports are doing their best to change matters. Black athletes, tennis players and rugby

Right: The South African born runner Zola Budd (number 151) found a fast route to British citizenship so that she would be eligible to compete in the Los Angeles Olympics.

players are being encouraged to improve their skills and are being allowed to play at somewhere near the top level with their white compatriots. But such opportunities are severely limited.

The white-run South African Cricket Union is also trying to make its sport multi-racial. The managing director, Ali Bacher, says: 'In two years we have introduced about 60,000 children under the age of fourteen to cricket – most of them black. We have taught more than 1,000 black teachers to be cricket coaches. We hold year-long clinics in all the major townships.'

But many people are suspicious of this frenzy of activity, and see it simply as a desperate attempt to impress foreign critics. Sam Ramsamy, chairman of SANROC, does not believe the figures given by Dr Bacher, nor does he believe that many Africans want to play cricket anyway! 'Unlike West Indians,' he says, 'there is no inherent appeal in the game for Africans, and children are being forced to the crease. The one reason they (the South African Cricket Union) are doing this is to try to find a passport for international acceptance.'

There is no doubt that the international ban hurts sportsmen and sportswomen, who have no chance to measure themselves against foreign competition. The runner Zola Budd seemed to have escaped the ban. Although born in South Africa, she was eligible for British citizenship and in 1984 she was granted this much more quickly than most people seeking such a status, and just in time for her to run in the Olympic Games. Her opponents were angry that she had been given preferential treatment and that she should be allowed to run for Britain when no-one (least of all the athlete herself) really thought that she was anything other than a South African. Eventually, when her career as a runner seemed to have come to a halt, Zola Budd went home.

Sportsmen and sportswomen from other countries who ignore the ban and compete in South Africa do so for any number of reasons. Some may be offered a lot of money; they argue that because sport in South Africa is becoming more integrated, they are justified in going. Some sincerely believe that they are doing good by playing multi-racial sport. Others argue that the boycott restricts their freedom as individuals to travel where they please. They ignore the fact that millions of black South Africans suffer much more serious restrictions to their movements; forced to live sometimes hundreds of miles from their work, they may see their families only once or twice a year.

The debate continues, and will do so until apartheid is abolished in South Africa. Over the last few years there have been some reforms to the system and it may be that the sporting boycott has encouraged this. Whether or not that is the case, many people feel very strongly that to play sport in South Africa is to support the system of apartheid, and they are not prepared to do that.

Racism around the world

> If I win I am an American, not a black American; if I did something bad, they would call me a Negro.
> *Tommie Smith, American athlete*

Tommie Smith had just won the 200 metres at the Olympic Games in Mexico in 1968. He had smashed the world record and proved himself to be one of the greatest sprinters in athletics history. Now he was standing on the rostrum waiting to receive his gold medal.

But, with the medal dangling on his chest and the American national anthem blaring out, Smith did an extraordinary thing. He lowered his head and raised his fist, which was encased in a black leather glove. He was giving the salute of the Black Power movement, which was fighting for equal rights for black people in the USA. For this, he was sent home early in disgrace. In the years that followed, Smith received more than fifty death threats, was spat on in the street, and was hounded out of sport.

Right: Tommie Smith and his American teammate giving the Black Power salute on the Olympic rostrum after being awarded the gold and bronze medals respectively for the 200 metres in the Mexico City Games in 1968.

We should not forget that racism is found in other countries of the world besides South Africa. There is nothing new in this. As long ago as 1908, Jack Johnson became the first great black sports star when he won a fight for the world heavyweight boxing championship. But at home in the USA he was hated and jeered, simply because of his colour. In 1957, Althea Gibson shrugged off racial insults and discouragement to win tennis titles at New York and Wimbledon.

Today it is much easier for black American sportsmen and sportswomen to break through the barriers of racial prejudice. Yet the opportunities to become real stars are hard to find. Apart from athletes, boxers, football and basketball players, there are very few black people at the top of the sporting ladder. Even American football, which owes so much to its black

Black and white baseball players now play in the same teams throughout America, but until 1947 blacks were excluded from Major League teams. They had their own league and the two leagues did not meet.

heroes, has yet to see a top-class black player at quarter-back, the key position on the field.

This same lack of sporting opportunity for racial minorities can be found in other countries too. Australian aboriginals and New Zealand Maoris rarely reach stardom on the sportsfield. We remember great players, such as tennis champion Evonne Goolagong and rugby back Mark Ella, partly because they were outstanding performers and partly because they came from unusual backgrounds. But their achievements have helped to bring renewed pride and hope to their peoples.

5 Playing for glory

New Zealand is a young country, with a population only half the size of London's. It is not a major world power, and has produced few notable artists, writers or statesmen. Yet it is without doubt the best rugby-playing nation in the world.

Since the Second World War it has scarcely been challenged for the unofficial title of world champion. Between 1953 and 1967, for example, the New Zealand 'All Blacks' toured the United Kingdom three times. The combined score sheet reads: won 63, lost 3! The New Zealanders confirmed their supremacy in 1987 when they won Rugby Union's very first World Cup. Not only did they conquer all other teams – they beat them easily.

Success on the rugby pitch has brought much pleasure and pride to New Zealand. The glory of winning well adds greatly to the confidence of the whole nation. In rugby terms, at least, New Zealanders stand tall over much bigger rivals, such as Australia, France and England.

Success on the cricket field has produced the same kind of self-respect and enthusiasm in the people of the Caribbean. Since 1976, the West Indies team has thrashed the rest of the world – particularly the English, who invented the game. Between 1984 and 1988, the West

Below: The New Zealand rugby team, the All Blacks, are a source of pride to their country.

Viv Richards, who made his Test debut in 1974, is one of a long line of exciting batsmen to come from the West Indies.

Indians defeated England fourteen times in fifteen matches, often by massive margins. The last time England beat them at home was way back in 1969.

The West Indies is not just the most successful team in the world, it is also the most exciting. Its great line of batsmen, from Learie Constantine through Garfield Sobers to Viv Richards, has thrilled crowds around the world, with flamboyant, attacking play. And in recent years, opposing players have been terrified by express bowlers such as Michael Holding and Malcolm Marshall.

It is extraordinary that such talent should have emerged from a handful of small islands scattered in the Caribbean. Antigua, for example, is a tiny speck in the ocean with a population of only 80,000. Yet it has produced two of the finest cricketers of all time in Viv Richards and Andy Roberts.

West Indians feel an enormous pride in the achievements of their cricket team. This pride is not simply to do with bats and balls, but with politics in the widest sense. They will never forget that less than two centuries ago the black people of the Caribbean were slaves working for white Europeans. Now they are the foremost cricketing nation in the world, and teams from predominantly white countries shudder at the thought of facing them. Winning at cricket is one way of wiping out the past.

Out of the Third World

Until 1960 no black African had ever won a gold medal at the Olympics. Yet when Abebe Bikila came padding barefoot into the Rome stadium to win the marathon, it was the beginning of a sporting revolution. Bikila was an Ethiopian, and his native country was poor and little-known to the outside world. Now it was firmly on the Olympic map.

Bikila won the marathon again in 1964. Four years later, in Mexico, African runners swept the board in long-distance running. Mamo Wolde, another Ethiopian, won the marathon, while Mohammed Gammoudi of Tunisia won the 5,000 metres. Three Kenyans – Kipchoge Keino, Amos Biwott and Naftali Temu – shared the rest. And so the procession went on. In 1980 Miruts Yifter (Ethiopian yet again) joined the ranks of the immortals by winning both the 5,000 and 10,000 metres races. Said Aouita of Morocco astonished everyone with his 5,000 metres victory in 1984. Over the next three years he set new world records for three separate distances.

Within a few years, Africa has leapt from nowhere into the forefront of athletics. But why had it not happened before? Africans were obviously very talented athletes. Why had they taken so long to establish themselves? One reason was that there is no tradition in Africa of

The Ethiopian Abebe Bikila winning his second Olympic marathon at the Tokyo games in 1964.

competing at sports, and few organized games. The other, political, reason was that until the late 1950s, much of the continent was ruled by the colonial powers of Europe. Native Africans were not encouraged to take up sports, as they were in the West Indies and India.

Why then did Africa explode so swiftly on to the scene after 1960? Again, there are two reasons, and both of them are political. The first is that countries like Kenya and Morocco became independent states freed from colonial rule. With independence came a national identity and pride, which encouraged national sports. The second reason is that many of these newly independent nations were given expert coaching by Soviet and other trainers from the Communist world. By giving their help free, the Soviets hoped to increase their influence in the continent.

The feats of Bikila, Keino, Yifter and others have made them heroes to the emerging nations of Africa. Sport has brought pride and glory to people who sometimes have little else to cheer about, especially in the drought-stricken areas of the north and east. Sport has also helped to unite the African nations, such as when twenty-two of them boycotted the 1976 Olympic Games in protest at the New Zealand rugby team's tour of South Africa.

> African men, many hundreds and thousands of them, spend much of their mobile life running. It could only be a matter of time in the twentieth century before Africans started running for sport.
> *Sebastian Coe and Nicholas Mason,*
> The Olympians

Below: Kipchoge Keino leaping the water jump in the 3,000 metres steeplechase at the Munich Olympics in 1972. His victory proved that African long-distance runners are among the best in the world.

Prestige and politics

Politicians are proud of their sports stars. They want them to win, because winning brings glory – and that glory will be reflected back on the politicians themselves. In some cases, this is no bad thing. As we have seen, the sporting triumphs of small and emerging countries like the West Indies, Ethiopia and New Zealand are important boosts to national morale. In the same way, Brazilians take great pride in their footballers and motor racing drivers, and Austrians idolize their downhill skiers.

But this lust for glory often gets out of hand. The bigger the nation, it seems, the more important victory becomes. The biggest nations today, in terms of strength, are the so-called superpowers, the USA and the Soviet Union. And they both want to win, very badly.

These two nations have been rivals in a 'cold war' for more than forty years. They are divided by their political beliefs. The Americans stand for the capitalist way of life, with freedom of speech, freedom to make money, and democratic government. The Soviets stand for the Marxist ideals of socialism, with central state control and the equal division of wealth.

The USA and the USSR have not actually gone into battle against each other, but they have expressed their antagonism to each other in the build-up of huge armies, the manufacturing of nuclear weapons, the encouragement of

revolution in smaller nations and the skul-duggery of the secret services. Victories in this kind of war are few and far between. On the sports field, however, they are easier to find – and more obvious.

The East–West sports war has been going on ever since 1952, when the USSR entered the Olympics for the first time. Nationality is not supposed to matter at the Games: every athlete competes as an individual, not as a representative of this or that country. But as far as the Americans and the Soviets were concerned, nationalism was all-important. Not for the first time, the Olympics had become a stage for political rivalry.

The rivalry has continued ever since. During each Games an unofficial medals table is drawn up, to find out which nation has been the overall 'winner'. In spite of the fact that it goes directly against the original Olympic spirit, the table is closely examined by those who are most likely to be at the top – that is, the Americans, the Soviet Union and their allies, the East Germans.

Below: The political rivalry between the USA and the USSR gives added excitement to any sporting meeting between them. Here their ice hockey teams compete in the 1980 Winter Olympics.

Even outside athletics, the competition is fierce between East and West. The most controversial moment of all came during a basketball match in 1972. The USA, which had never been beaten at the game, was leading 50–49 when the final hooter sounded. But officials ruled that an extra three seconds must be added. In that time the Soviet team managed to score again and win. Tempers flared, and there were accusations of cheating.

Another source of Western anger is the intensive coaching methods of the communist nations. The Soviet Union and East Germany make no secret of their state-run schemes. Budding athletes, gymnasts and skaters are spotted early and sent to special training schools, where the best of them are carefully groomed to become champions. The success of this scheme is obvious: the USSR has gained most medals in every Olympics it has entered (except for 1968), and is world leader in many other sports.

American and Western European critics have mocked this system of training. They compare it to 'conveyor belts' and 'state fish farms', and Western newspapers carry stories with headlines such as 'Automatons Who Do Not Laugh' and 'Russia's Broiler-Bred Athletes'. A famous television commentator once said of East German athletes: 'They are all programmed from conception to the grave.'

Remarks like these reveal a great deal of ignorance and, perhaps, some jealousy of Communist triumphs. Of course, the Soviet Union

The suppleness and grace of the Rumanian Aurelia Dobrai and other Eastern European gymnasts has amazed millions. However, the intensive training necessary to achieve such elasticity can lead to problems such as crippling arthritis in later life.

may be too obsessed with winning at games and showing itself superior to the West. But are American athletes, with their wealthy sponsors and well-equipped colleges, really any different? Certainly gymnasts from both East and West pay a high price for their dedication to sport. From an early age they spend many hours doing tough training routines which bend their bodies and strain ligaments and muscles. All too often the result of this in later life is arthritis, rheumatism and other crippling pains.

6 Women in the spotlight

Women have but one task, that of crowning the winner with garlands.
Baron Pierre de Coubertin, 1902

I came out here to beat everybody in sight, and that is exactly what I'm going to do.
Mildred 'Babe' Didrikson, double gold medallist at the 1932 Olympic Games

The twentieth century has seen an astonishing change in the place of women in society. Their fight for equal pay, equal opportunities and equal rights has been fierce and determined (though it is not over yet by a long way). It has had little to do with governments or political parties, but all the same it has been a political struggle in the widest sense. And sport has been an essential part of it.

Women today have a prominent share in the glamorous world of international sport. But they have had to climb a mountain of male prejudice to get it. In 1900, few people took women's sports seriously. There was only one women's event at the Olympic Games that year, and it was tennis. Tennis was considered to be a slow and ladylike game. The players wore long, heavy skirts, petticoats, corsets and sometimes big straw hats.

Then in the 1920s a female whirlwind swept all this away. Suzanne Lenglen played in short skirts and no corsets. Her arms were bare, and she ran and leapt about the court like a deer. The staid Wimbledon spectators were shocked, but Lenglen quickly proved herself to be the most brilliant tennis player in the world. Her matches soon drew bigger crowds

In 1918 women were expected to play tennis in long skirts which restricted their movement.

Right: Suzanne Lenglen, in the 1920s, shocked people with her short shirt and bare arms, but she beat all the other women with ease.

than any played by men.

Elsewhere, women were showing in dramatic ways that they too could be great athletes. In 1926 Gertrude Ederle became the first woman to swim the English Channel. She broke the existing record time (set by a man) by two hours. In 1932, Mildred 'Babe' Didrikson, short-haired, muscular and determined, won two Olympic gold medals in athletics and shared a third. Sonja Henie, the first superstar of the skating rink, was unbeaten between 1927 and 1936 at figure skating.

Gertrude Ederle, covered in grease to protect her from the cold, shaking hands with a fellow swimmer before embarking on her record-breaking swim across the English Channel in 1926.

Left: The javelin thrower Fatima Whitbread is proud of her muscles, which some consider to be 'un-feminine'.

There have been outstanding women in these sports, and many others, ever since. Suzanne Lenglen has been followed by great champions like Billie-Jean King and Martina Navratilova. 'Babe' Didrikson has been followed by a host of spectacular record-breakers, culminating in the extraordinary feats of Florence Griffith-Joyner. Sonja Henie has been followed by world-famous skaters such as Katarina Witt, the undoubted sensation of the 1988 Winter Olympics in Calgary.

Women can also take the credit for turning some of the less popular sports into headline news. The most notable example of this is gymnastics. It was a respectable enough event until 1972, when a tiny Soviet gymnast called Olga Korbut captured the hearts of millions of television viewers with her performance in the Munich Olympics. Four years later, Nadia Comaneci won three gold medals and a bronze, and astonished everyone by becoming the first Olympic gymnast to gain a perfect score of 10.00.

All these champions have conclusively shown that women are not to be dismissed as 'the weaker sex'. On the contrary, they are capable of many physical achievements which might have made their grandmothers faint with shock. The examples set by the great athletes have inspired millions of ordinary women to take up games for themselves. Sport has given them the freedom and opportunity to change their lives.

Not suitable for women?

People think of me as the incredible hulk. I don't dislike my muscles. I enjoy feeling healthy, looking good.
Fatima Whitbread, British javelin thrower

The 3,000 metres race is a little too strenuous for women.
International Olympic Committee, 1978

This win is a triumph for women's athletics.
Joan Benoit, gold medallist in the first women's Olympic marathon, 1984

1928 should have been a great year for women's liberation in sport. For the very first time, the Olympic Games included athletics events for women. Before this, athletics had been considered far too dangerous and unsuitable for females. Now they were to compete in the 100 metres, the high jump, the discus and the relay.

Joan Benoit of the USA in 1984, after winning the first women's Olympic marathon.

But it was the fifth event which worried the International Olympic Committee. This was the 800 metres. Could women, they wondered, possibly be strong enough to run that far? Lina Radke of Germany proved that they could, winning the gold medal after a determined race. Unfortunately, some of the other runners seemed to collapse as they crossed the tape, and the damage was done. The women's 800 metres was abandoned, and was not to reappear until 1960.

It has taken the IOC an amazingly long time to recognize that women are just as capable as men of doing strenuous things with their bodies. The 400 metres for women was first included in 1964, the 1,500 metres in 1972 and the 10,000 metres in 1988. The biggest triumph of all for female athletes was the first Olympic marathon, run at Los Angeles in 1984. This killing race, over 42.295 km (26 miles, 385 yards), was won by Joan Benoit.

Benoit, along with other legendary marathon runners, such as Greta Waitz and Ingrid Kristiansen, had made another great breakthrough. Women rapidly began following their examples and running marathons, half-marathons and family fun-runs. The running revolution was attracting women in just as huge numbers as men, so that today there are over 100,000 female marathon runners in the USA alone.

The long struggle to have women's long distance races included in international games is not simply to do with medals and records. The struggle is really against what people expect from women. Women are supposed to be pretty, feminine, home-loving and rather weak. They are not expected to be plain, muscular, strong and dedicated to sporting careers.

Women have been making their mark in many other sports which were once thought to be too un-feminine or dangerous for them. Fatima Whitbread developed a mass of muscles which enabled her to hurl a javelin to a new world record. Virginia Holgate Leng rode her horse against men in the perilous, and sometimes fatal, world of three-day eventing. Once, she fell and broke her arm in twenty-three places. But she recovered to become European Champion in 1985 and World Champion in 1986.

Below: Virginia Leng takes part in the only sport in which women compete against men.

7 Sport without politics?

Athleticism can occasion the most noble passions or the most vile; it can develop impartiality and the feeling of honour, as can love of winning. It can be chivalrous or corrupt, vile, bestial. One can use it to consolidate peace or prepare for war.
Baron Pierre de Coubertin

Look around the world today and you can be left in no doubt: sport and politics are tangled up more tightly than ever before. The Olympic Games have become the scene of boycotts, disharmony and even bloodshed. The major cricketing nations squabble about contacts with South Africa. East and West use sportsmen and sportswomen as soldiers in their long-running 'cold war'.

Nor is there any doubt that sport suffers badly from all this. International competitions are spoiled or cancelled. The desperate need to win at all costs leads to scandals over drug abuse and other forms of cheating. Boycotts and bans prevent brilliant sportsmen and sportswomen from appearing on the world stage.

Clearly, it is a sad state of affairs. But can sport ever be separated from politics? The International Olympic Committee certainly works hard to try and keep its regular Games free from political interference. We have seen in previous chapters how it very often fails. Yet in many ways it succeeds. Young athletes from hundreds of different countries meet and learn more about each other. Records are broken and great feats are performed.

Below: The riot at the Heysel Stadium in 1985, during which English and Italian football hooligans fought each other and thirty-nine Italians died, showed the worst face of nationalism.

The Australian team, in 'national costume', taking part in the opening ceremony of the 1988 Seoul Olympics. As long as the Olympic Games continues to be an arena for displays of national pride, it will be impossible to separate it from international politics.

One obvious way of excluding politics from the Olympics would be to discourage displays of nationalism. Competitors are supposed to be individuals and not representatives of teams, so why do they parade about under their nations' flags? And why are national anthems played at medal ceremonies? Many IOC members have been unhappy about this, including Lord Killanin: 'I am opposed to nationalism, and I would be happier if national anthems were not used at the Games, but I realize that my view is not that of the majority.'

Measures like this might improve the atmosphere in the athletics stadium, but what about team sports? Football, hockey, basketball, volleyball and ice hockey matches deliberately pit one nation against another. Spectators come to cheer for their countrymen. It is not at all surprising that patriotism soon turns into unpleasant chauvinism.

But if sport cannot be separated from politics, what about the sportsmen and sportswomen themselves? Few of them are politicians. All they want is to carry on training and competing in peace, without interference from governments or pressure groups. It is hard to expect them to be champions and diplomats at one and the same time. Sport, they insist, should be left alone.

All the same, the sports stars have to realize that all their actions are very public, and can influence the thinking of ordinary people. When cricketer Ian Botham was offered a huge sum of money to play in South Africa, he refused. He said that if he accepted he would never be able to look his West Indian friends in the face again.

Botham was making a clear point about South Africa and its system of apartheid. South Africa is a deeply unpopular country, and fewer and fewer sports stars now have contact with it. But is the behaviour of the South African government any worse than the behaviour of other politicians? What about the USSR, with its suppression of free speech and its invasion of Afghanistan? Or the USA, with its sinister meddling in Latin America? Or Zaire and Paraguay, with their harsh dictatorships? Athletes have some hard decisions to make.

Signs of hope

Sportsmen usually look at politics from their own special point of view. They see that politics damages sport. But if they tried the politician's point of view, they might see a rosier picture. International sport surely has a positive contribution to make to world affairs.

First of all, games encourage people from different nations, colours and religious backgrounds to meet each other. They travel to each other's countries, learn about new ways of living, and make new friendships.

Secondly, sport teaches people to work together in teams. They learn to co-operate with their fellows if they want to be effective. Teams do not have to be divided up by nationality. In English county cricket and League soccer, for example, players from several different countries and creeds may be working together towards a common target.

Thirdly, the stars of international sport can inspire ordinary people to take up games themselves. The success of Olga Korbut and Nadia Comaneci sparked off a gymnastics revolution, and millions began running marathons after watching Joan Benoit and Greta Waitz. People who are active and fit are usually happier for it.

Finally, sport is an area of certainty in an uncertain world. Politicians and other powerful people often deal in lies and deception. But athletes cannot do that (particularly in these days of super-sensitive drug detection techniques). The fastest man in the world is the runner who holds the 100 metres world record. The best woman tennis player in the world is the one who wins most championship matches. The best football team wins the World Cup. There is no arguing with these statements; they are facts. And this certainty is a source of confidence for many people.

If politics were like a sporting event, there would be several virtues to attach to its name: clarity, honesty, excellence.
Neil Postman, Amusing Ourselves to Death *1985*

The Olympic Movement is not just about siting and organizing a super sports competition every four years, but has the ideal of bringing people together in peace regardless of race, religion and colour.
Lord Killanin, IOC President 1972–80

Below: The London Marathon attracts top athletes as well as people who may be running their first race. It also has a large number of entrants in racing wheelchairs.

Glossary

Aboriginals The first race of people to settle in Australia, about 40,000 years ago.

Apartheid The policy of separating the different races within a country, practised by the South African government.

Aryans An ancient people who spoke an early version of European languages. Hitler mistakenly defined Aryans as a white, non-Jewish race, descended from Nordic tribes.

Black Power Movement A movement among black Americans, aiming at social equality and political power for Negroes.

Boycott To stop dealing or playing with another nation (as a way of protesting).

British Empire The collection of countries which were once under British colonial rule. The Empire was at its height in the nineteenth century.

Cape coloured A South African of mixed race who lives near the Cape Peninsula.

Capitalism An economic system based on free competition and the building up of private wealth.

Celebrity tournaments Sporting competitions in which famous players take part alongside stars from other walks of life, for example, film actors and politicians.

Centenary A celebration one hundred years after an event.

Chauvinism A belief that one's own nation or group is superior to any other.

Citizenship The official status of belonging to a nation, with all the rights and privileges that go with that status.

Cold war A state of rivalry and tension between nations which stops short of actual fighting.

Concentration camp A prison camp in which political prisoners or aliens are kept together.

Downhill skiing A skiing event in which competitors race one at a time down a slope against the clock.

Grand Prix races A series of motor races over international tracks which count towards the drivers' annual world championship.

Indigenous people Those originating in a country, rather than people who settled there from another country.

Maori A member of the Maori tribe, the first race to settle in New Zealand.

Nationalism Excessively strong pride in one's nation and its interests.

Nazi A member of the National Socialist Party which, led by Hitler, ruled Germany from 1933 to 1945.

Propaganda News, posters, leaflets and other kinds of information which are published solely to support or discredit a particular cause or political view.

Slave Someone who is legally owned by another person and who has no rights.

Socialism A system of government in which goods, money, property and power are shared by the whole community.

Suez Canal Zone The area around the major shipping canal which connects the Mediterranean and Red Seas. It was the scene of conflict in 1956 when the Egyptians claimed ownership.

Swastika The emblem of Nazi Germany.

Books to read

Blue, Adrianne, *Faster, Higher, Further: Women's Triumphs and Disasters at the Olympics* (Virago, 1988)

Booker, Christopher, *The Games War: Moscow 1980* (Faber, 1981)

Coe, Sebastian, *The Olympians* (Pavilion, 1988)

Hart-Davis, Duff, *Hitler's Games* (Century, 1986)

James, C.L.R., *Beyond a Boundary* (Hutchinson, 1963)

Killanin, 3rd Baron, and Rodda, John, *The Olympic Games* (Macdonald & Janes, 1980)

Matthews, Peter and Morrison, Ian, *The Guinness Encyclopedia of Sports Records and Results* (Guinness, 1987)

Riordan, James, *Soviet Sport* (Blackwell, 1980)

Soar, Phil and Tyler, Martin, *The Story of Football* (Hamlyn, 1986)

Picture acknowledgements

Allsport: cover (Simon Bruty), 6 (Dave Stock), 9, 10, 14 (top) (Adrian Murrell), 15 (Russell Cheyne), 17 (top), 19 (bottom), 23 (David Cannon), 26 (Adrian Murrell), 31 (Russell Cheyne), 32 (Adrian Murrell), 34 (Steve Powell), 35 (Bob Martin), 40 (Tony Duffy), 41 (Bob Martin); Colorsport 25, 30 (Focus-West), 43; Hulton Picture Company 13, 36, 39; The Billie Love Collection 11; Popperfoto: frontispiece, 14 (bottom), 19 (top), 29, 33 (bottom); Rex Features 20, 21, 24; Sefton Photo Library 16, 33 (top), 38; Frank Spooner Pictures 7, 22, 27, 42, 44; Topham 17 (bottom), 18, 37; Western Americana 12.

Further information

British Olympic Association
1 Wandsworth Plain
London SW18

The Rt-Hon. Minister for Sport
Department of the Environment
2 Marsham St
London SW1P

Women's Amateur Athletics Association
Francis House
Francis St
London SW1P

The Anti-Apartheid Movement
13 Selous St
London NW1

The Southern African Committee
United Nations Organization
17 West 17th St, 8th Floor
New York 10011
USA

Australia
Australian Olympic Federation
67 Palmerston Crescent
South Melbourne
VIC 3205

and

157 Gloucester Street
Sydney
NSW 2000

Australian Institute of Sport
Curtin Campus
PO Box 144
Como
WA 6152

and

Old Cleveland Road
Brisbane
QLD 4000

New Zealand

NZ Olympic and Commonwealth
   Games Association Inc
59 Cambridge Terrace
Wellington

NZ Rugby Football Union Inc
Huddart Parker Building
Post Office Square
Wellington

Canada

Canadian Olympic Association
333 River Road
Tower 'R', 13th Floor
Vanier
Ontario K1L 8H9

Fitness and Amateur Sport Canada
Journal Tower South
365 Laurier Avenue West
Ottawa
Ontario K1A 0X6

Index